CHEETAH

BY TYLER GRADY

Dylanna Press

Cheetahs

Cheetahs are **mammals** that mainly live in Africa south of the Sahara Desert. Small populations of cheetahs live in North Africa and Iran.

There are five subspecies of cheetahs including Tanzanian (also known as Kenyan or East African), Sudan, South African, Northwest African, and Asiatic cheetahs.

They are related to lions, tigers, leopards, jaguars, and other types of big cats. Their scientific name is *Acinonyx jubatus* and they belong to the Felidae family.

---

mammals – warm-blooded animals with hair or fur that give birth to live young

One of the most recognizable members of the animal kingdom, cheetahs are known for their incredible speed and distinctive spots. They are the fastest land animals on earth!

Adults weigh between 45 to 160 pounds (20 to 72.5 kg) and average 3 1/2 to 5 feet (1 to 1.5 m) in length with a long tail of 2 to 3 feet (65 to 85 cm). Males are slightly larger than females.

Cheetahs are tall and slender with long, thin legs. Their coats are light tan to dark golden with solid black spots. They also have distinctive black stripes running from the inside corner of their eyes to their mouths. The ends of their tails are bushy with black rings.

Cheetahs can live in a range of **habitats** including grasslands, savannahs, shrublands, and deserts. They tend to prefer open grasslands with lots of space to utilize their amazing speed.

Cheetahs were once common throughout Africa, Asia, and Europe but they have unfortunately lost more than 90 percent of their historical range. This is due to a combination of reasons including game hunting and human settlement.

---

habitat – surroundings or conditions in which an animal lives

The cheetah has many physical adaptations to its environment.

Their fur acts as **camouflage**, helping them to blend in to the environment. Their distinctive "tear marks" help protect their eyes from the sun's glare.

Cheetahs are built for speed. They possess light skeletons, long and lean muscles, spring-like ligaments, and oversized heart and lungs that allows them to take in large amounts of oxygen for sprinting. Their long muscular tails help them keep balance when running at high speeds.

---

adaptations – ways in which a species becomes fitted into its natural environment to increase its chance of survival

camouflage – a mechanism used to disguise appearance

Cheetahs are **carnivores**. Their preferred food source is small- to medium-sized **herbivores** such as gazelles and antelopes. In addition, they will also eat smaller mammals such as rabbits and even birds.

Cheetahs typically do not eat every day. They will consume between 6 to 8 pounds (2.7 to 3.6 kg) at once and then go 2 to 5 days before hunting again. They eat only fresh meat and will not scavenge or eat **carrion**.

Since watering holes tend to be scarce where cheetahs live, they only drink every 3 to 4 days and get the rest of their water from their prey.

---

carnivore – animal that only eats meat

herbivore – animal that eats plants

carrion – dead and decaying animal

Cheetahs have large home ranges, up to 300 square miles (800 sq. km). They travel long distances hunting migratory prey animals.

They hunt by stalking and creeping up on their prey, only using their speed to give chase when they get as close as possible. They are able to accelerate very quickly and attack by grabbing their target's legs, making them fall. Reaching speeds of up to 80 miles per hour (130 km per hour), cheetah's are successful about 50 percent of the time in catching their prey.

Cheetahs typically hunt alone. The exception is groups of young related males who will form **coalitions** of 2 to 5 members and will hunt larger animals together.

---

coalition – small group of cheetahs

Cheetahs are **polygamous**, with both males and females mating with more than one partner. Mating can take place at any time of year. Cheetahs reach maturity between 1 1/2 to 2 years old.

After conception takes place, the male cheetah leaves and has nothing to do with the female or her future cubs.

Pregnancy lasts an average of 93 days and female cheetahs typically give birth to between two to five cubs at a time.

_____

polygamous – having more than one mate at a time

Baby cheetahs are called

cubs. They are born blind and helpless. The mother cheetah takes care of them by herself, keeping them safe and providing food. She moves them every couple of days to try and avoid predators.

When the mother cheetah goes out to hunt the cubs are left alone, sometimes for long periods. During this time they are very vulnerable and as high as 90 percent do not survive. After about six weeks cubs are be able to go out with their mother.

Cubs grow rapidly, reaching half their adult size by 6 months and able to start hunting by 8 months. By the time they are 18 months, young cheetahs are ready to go out into the world on their own.

Cheetahs love to sleep! They average about 12 hours per day. This is needed to preserve and recharge their energy levels. They tend to rest in the shady area beneath trees or in tall grasses. They do not use dens.

Unlike most other big cats cheetahs are **diurnal**. They are most active in the morning and late afternoon and sleep at night. Since their night vision is not any better than humans, they need daylight in order to hunt.

---

diurnal – awake and active during the day

21

Female adults are **solitary** animals who spend the majority of their lives alone, with the exception of a mother cheetah and her cubs. Adult males tend to form small groups that live and hunt together. Males and females only interact during mating.

Unlike other big cats, cheetahs do not roar. They communicate through other types of **vocalizations** such as growls, hisses, and purrs.

Male, but not female, cheetahs are **territorial** and will defend a range large enough to provide them with an adequate supply of food. A female cheetah will roam across several male cheetahs' territory.

To mark their territory, cheetahs will leave scent marks and scratches on trees.

---

solitary – done or existing alone

vocalizations – the sounds an animal makes

territorial – an animal that defends a specific area of land

The average lifespan of a cheetah in the wild is 10 to 12 years. Males tend to die sooner due to confilcts over territory with competing coalitions. They can live up to 20 years in captivity.

Scientists estimate that there are currently only 7,100 cheetahs left in the wild. This is a drastic decline from the estimated 100,000 cheetahs living 100 years ago.

Cheetahs are currently listed as a **vulnerable species** but due to severe population declines they may soon be considered an endangered species.

_____

vulnerable species – species considered to be facing a high risk of extinction in the wild

While predators themselves, cheetahs are also **prey** to other animals such as lions, leopards, and hyenas. Cheetah cubs are the most vulnerable to predation with fewer than 1 in 10 surviving to adulthood.

Humans are the biggest threats to cheetahs. Habit destruction and climate change are forcing cheetahs into smaller territories with less food sources available.

In addition, cheetahs are hunted both to protect livestock and also for trophies. Illegal smuggling for the exotic pet trade is another threat to their survival in the wild.

---

prey – animal that is hunted and killed by another animal for food

Cheetahs are beautiful and exotic animals. As the fastest animals on earth, they are symbols of speed and agility.

Unfortunately, cheetahs continued existence is in doubt due to loss of habitat, hunting, and illegal capture of cubs.

Conservation efforts are underway but it remains to be seen if this amazing big cat can survive in the coming decades.

---

conservation – protecting natural resources for future generations

Word Search

```
E I S U H Q E T E R R I T O R Y
L A N R U I D X R O T A D E R P
Y S P E C I E S T H P F J H A L
R M W C G T E G C I U E O Y Z A
A N W A D B Z M O C N N Z C O Z
T E T R X D I M N F H C T U H I
I G T N O E E Q S U A E T I R N
L A A I H R T T E W P S E I N A
O L T V V E V L R R H L T T O G
S F I O D L A L V D F I M E A N
U U B R D M B K A D T F T Y S H
F O A E M S U O T V F E T Q Q T
T M H A I A Y R I N H S E T K K
D A M Q U I P K O L C P X N H C
Q C V U Q Y L K N O W A K M H I
C N O I T A T P A D A N G Q S E
```

ADAPTATION	CONSERVATION	HABITAT	PREDATOR
CAMOUFLAGE	DIURNAL	HUNTING	SOLITARY
CARNIVORE	EXTINCTION	LIFESPAN	SPECIES
CHEETAH	FASTEST	MAMMAL	TERRITORY

INDEX

Acinonyx jubatus, 4
adaptations, 11
camouflage, 11
carnivores, 12
carrion, 12
classification, 4
climate change, 27
coalitions, 15, 24
conservation, 28
cubs, 16, 19, 27
description, 7
diet, 12
diurnal, 20
Felidae family, 4
food, 12
grasslands, 8
habitat, 4, 8
habitat destruction, 27, 28
herbivores, 12
hunting, 8, 15, 27, 28
lifespan, 24
mammals, 4
mating, 16

mothers, 19
night vision, 20
parenting, 19
physical appearance, 7, 11
polygamous, 16
population, 24
predators, 27
pregnancy, 16
prey, 27
range, 8, 15, 23
size, 7
sleep, 20
smuggling, 27
solitary, 23
speed, 11, 15
subspecies, 4
territory, 15, 23, 24
threats, 8, 27
vocalizations, 23
vulnerable species, 24
water, 12

Published by Dylanna Press an imprint of Dylanna Publishing, Inc.
Copyright © 2022 by Dylanna Press
Author: Tyler Grady

Printed in the U.S.A.

Made in the USA
Monee, IL
16 December 2024

74145195R00019